MY MONEY JOURNAL

AF808179

DATE:

COPYRIGHT © MARTINA PUBLISHING. INC.

MY MONEY JOURNAL

January ___________

DATE	ITEM DESCRIPTION	I OWE YOU	YOU OWE ME	PAID

NOTES:

MY MONEY JOURNAL

January ____________

DATE	ITEM DESCRIPTION	I OWE YOU	YOU OWE ME	PAID

NOTES:

MY MONEY JOURNAL

January ____________

DATE	ITEM DESCRIPTION	I OWE YOU	YOU OWE ME	PAID

NOTES:

MY MONEY JOURNAL

January ____________

DATE	ITEM DESCRIPTION	I OWE YOU	YOU OWE ME	PAID

NOTES:

MY MONEY JOURNAL

January ____________

DATE	ITEM DESCRIPTION	I OWE YOU	YOU OWE ME	PAID

NOTES:

MY MONEY JOURNAL

January ____________

DATE	ITEM DESCRIPTION	I OWE YOU	YOU OWE ME	PAID

NOTES:

MY MONEY JOURNAL

January ___________

DATE	ITEM DESCRIPTION	I OWE YOU	YOU OWE ME	PAID

NOTES:

MY MONEY JOURNAL

January ____________

DATE	ITEM DESCRIPTION	I OWE YOU	YOU OWE ME	PAID

NOTES:

____

____

____

____

____

____

MY MONEY JOURNAL

January ____________

DATE	ITEM DESCRIPTION	I OWE YOU	YOU OWE ME	PAID

NOTES:

MY MONEY JOURNAL

February ____________

DATE	ITEM DESCRIPTION	I OWE YOU	YOU OWE ME	PAID

NOTES:

____

____

____

____

____

____

MY MONEY JOURNAL

February ___________

DATE	ITEM DESCRIPTION	I OWE YOU	YOU OWE ME	PAID

NOTES:

MY MONEY JOURNAL

February ___________

DATE	ITEM DESCRIPTION	I OWE YOU	YOU OWE ME	PAID

NOTES:

MY MONEY JOURNAL

February ___________

DATE	ITEM DESCRIPTION	I OWE YOU	YOU OWE ME	PAID

NOTES:

MY MONEY JOURNAL

February ____________

DATE	ITEM DESCRIPTION	I OWE YOU	YOU OWE ME	PAID

NOTES:

MY MONEY JOURNAL

February ____________

DATE	ITEM DESCRIPTION	I OWE YOU	YOU OWE ME	PAID

NOTES:

MY MONEY JOURNAL

February ___________

DATE	ITEM DESCRIPTION	I OWE YOU	YOU OWE ME	PAID

NOTES:

MY MONEY JOURNAL

February ___________

DATE	ITEM DESCRIPTION	I OWE YOU	YOU OWE ME	PAID

NOTES:

MY MONEY JOURNAL

February ___________

DATE	ITEM DESCRIPTION	I OWE YOU	YOU OWE ME	PAID

NOTES:

MY MONEY JOURNAL

March ____________

DATE	ITEM DESCRIPTION	I OWE YOU	YOU OWE ME	PAID

NOTES:

MY MONEY JOURNAL

March ____________

DATE	ITEM DESCRIPTION	I OWE YOU	YOU OWE ME	PAID

NOTES:

MY MONEY JOURNAL

March ____________

DATE	ITEM DESCRIPTION	I OWE YOU	YOU OWE ME	PAID

NOTES:

____

____

____

____

____

____

MY MONEY JOURNAL

March ____________

DATE	ITEM DESCRIPTION	I OWE YOU	YOU OWE ME	PAID

NOTES:

MY MONEY JOURNAL

March ____________

DATE	ITEM DESCRIPTION	I OWE YOU	YOU OWE ME	PAID

NOTES:

___

___

___

___

___

___

MY MONEY JOURNAL

March ____________

DATE	ITEM DESCRIPTION	I OWE YOU	YOU OWE ME	PAID

NOTES:

MY MONEY JOURNAL

March ____________

DATE	ITEM DESCRIPTION	I OWE YOU	YOU OWE ME	PAID

NOTES:

MY MONEY JOURNAL

March ______________

DATE	ITEM DESCRIPTION	I OWE YOU	YOU OWE ME	PAID

NOTES:

MY MONEY JOURNAL

March ____________

DATE	ITEM DESCRIPTION	I OWE YOU	YOU OWE ME	PAID

NOTES:

MY MONEY JOURNAL

March ____________

DATE	ITEM DESCRIPTION	I OWE YOU	YOU OWE ME	PAID

NOTES:

MY MONEY JOURNAL

March ___________

DATE	ITEM DESCRIPTION	I OWE YOU	YOU OWE ME	PAID

NOTES:

MY MONEY JOURNAL

April ____________

DATE	ITEM DESCRIPTION	I OWE YOU	YOU OWE ME	PAID

NOTES:

____

____

____

____

____

____

MY MONEY JOURNAL

April ___________

DATE	ITEM DESCRIPTION	I OWE YOU	YOU OWE ME	PAID

NOTES:

MY MONEY JOURNAL

April ___________

DATE	ITEM DESCRIPTION	I OWE YOU	YOU OWE ME	PAID

NOTES:

MY MONEY JOURNAL

April ____________

DATE	ITEM DESCRIPTION	I OWE YOU	YOU OWE ME	PAID

NOTES:

MY MONEY JOURNAL

April ____________

DATE	ITEM DESCRIPTION	I OWE YOU	YOU OWE ME	PAID

NOTES:

____

____

____

____

____

____

MY MONEY JOURNAL

April ______

DATE	ITEM DESCRIPTION	I OWE YOU	YOU OWE ME	PAID

NOTES:

MY MONEY JOURNAL

April ___________

DATE	ITEM DESCRIPTION	I OWE YOU	YOU OWE ME	PAID

NOTES:

MY MONEY JOURNAL

April ____________

DATE	ITEM DESCRIPTION	I OWE YOU	YOU OWE ME	PAID

NOTES:

MY MONEY JOURNAL

April ____________

DATE	ITEM DESCRIPTION	I OWE YOU	YOU OWE ME	PAID

NOTES:

MY MONEY JOURNAL

April ____________

DATE	ITEM DESCRIPTION	I OWE YOU	YOU OWE ME	PAID

NOTES:

MY MONEY JOURNAL

May__________

DATE	ITEM DESCRIPTION	I OWE YOU	YOU OWE ME	PAID

NOTES:

MY MONEY JOURNAL

May __________

DATE	ITEM DESCRIPTION	I OWE YOU	YOU OWE ME	PAID

NOTES:

____

____

____

____

____

____

MY MONEY JOURNAL

May ___________

DATE	ITEM DESCRIPTION	I OWE YOU	YOU OWE ME	PAID

NOTES:

MY MONEY JOURNAL

May ____________

DATE	ITEM DESCRIPTION	I OWE YOU	YOU OWE ME	PAID

NOTES:

MY MONEY JOURNAL

May ____________

DATE	ITEM DESCRIPTION	I OWE YOU	YOU OWE ME	PAID

NOTES:

MY MONEY JOURNAL

May__________

DATE	ITEM DESCRIPTION	I OWE YOU	YOU OWE ME	PAID

NOTES:

MY MONEY JOURNAL

May ____________

DATE	ITEM DESCRIPTION	I OWE YOU	YOU OWE ME	PAID

NOTES:

MY MONEY JOURNAL

May ____________

DATE	ITEM DESCRIPTION	I OWE YOU	YOU OWE ME	PAID

NOTES:

MY MONEY JOURNAL

May ___________

DATE	ITEM DESCRIPTION	I OWE YOU	YOU OWE ME	PAID

NOTES:

MY MONEY JOURNAL

May__________

DATE	ITEM DESCRIPTION	I OWE YOU	YOU OWE ME	PAID

NOTES:

MY MONEY JOURNAL

June ____________

DATE	ITEM DESCRIPTION	I OWE YOU	YOU OWE ME	PAID

NOTES:

MY MONEY JOURNAL

June ______________

DATE	ITEM DESCRIPTION	I OWE YOU	YOU OWE ME	PAID

NOTES:

____

____

____

____

____

____

MY MONEY JOURNAL

June ____________

DATE	ITEM DESCRIPTION	I OWE YOU	YOU OWE ME	PAID

NOTES:

MY MONEY JOURNAL

June ____________

DATE	ITEM DESCRIPTION	I OWE YOU	YOU OWE ME	PAID

NOTES:

MY MONEY JOURNAL

June ____________

DATE	ITEM DESCRIPTION	I OWE YOU	YOU OWE ME	PAID

NOTES:

____

____

____

____

____

____

MY MONEY JOURNAL

June ______________

DATE	ITEM DESCRIPTION	I OWE YOU	YOU OWE ME	PAID

NOTES:

MY MONEY JOURNAL

June ________

DATE	ITEM DESCRIPTION	I OWE YOU	YOU OWE ME	PAID

NOTES:

MY MONEY JOURNAL

June ____________

DATE	ITEM DESCRIPTION	I OWE YOU	YOU OWE ME	PAID

NOTES:

MY MONEY JOURNAL

June ______________

DATE	ITEM DESCRIPTION	I OWE YOU	YOU OWE ME	PAID

NOTES:

MY MONEY JOURNAL

June ________

DATE	ITEM DESCRIPTION	I OWE YOU	YOU OWE ME	PAID

NOTES:

MY MONEY JOURNAL

July ____________

DATE	ITEM DESCRIPTION	I OWE YOU	YOU OWE ME	PAID

NOTES:

MY MONEY JOURNAL

July ___________

DATE	ITEM DESCRIPTION	I OWE YOU	YOU OWE ME	PAID

NOTES:

MY MONEY JOURNAL

July ____________

DATE	ITEM DESCRIPTION	I OWE YOU	YOU OWE ME	PAID

NOTES:

MY MONEY JOURNAL

July ___________

DATE	ITEM DESCRIPTION	I OWE YOU	YOU OWE ME	PAID

NOTES:

MY MONEY JOURNAL

July ____________

DATE	ITEM DESCRIPTION	I OWE YOU	YOU OWE ME	PAID

NOTES:

MY MONEY JOURNAL

July ___________

DATE	ITEM DESCRIPTION	I OWE YOU	YOU OWE ME	PAID

NOTES:

MY MONEY JOURNAL

July __________

DATE	ITEM DESCRIPTION	I OWE YOU	YOU OWE ME	PAID

NOTES:

MY MONEY JOURNAL

July ___________

DATE	ITEM DESCRIPTION	I OWE YOU	YOU OWE ME	PAID

NOTES:

MY MONEY JOURNAL

July ____________

DATE	ITEM DESCRIPTION	I OWE YOU	YOU OWE ME	PAID

NOTES:

MY MONEY JOURNAL

July ___________

DATE	ITEM DESCRIPTION	I OWE YOU	YOU OWE ME	PAID

NOTES:

MY MONEY JOURNAL

August ______________

DATE	ITEM DESCRIPTION	I OWE YOU	YOU OWE ME	PAID

NOTES:

MY MONEY JOURNAL

August ____________

DATE	ITEM DESCRIPTION	I OWE YOU	YOU OWE ME	PAID

NOTES:

MY MONEY JOURNAL

August ____________

DATE	ITEM DESCRIPTION	I OWE YOU	YOU OWE ME	PAID

NOTES:

MY MONEY JOURNAL

August ___________

DATE	ITEM DESCRIPTION	I OWE YOU	YOU OWE ME	PAID

NOTES:

MY MONEY JOURNAL

August ______________

DATE	ITEM DESCRIPTION	I OWE YOU	YOU OWE ME	PAID

NOTES:

MY MONEY JOURNAL

August ____________

DATE	ITEM DESCRIPTION	I OWE YOU	YOU OWE ME	PAID

NOTES:

____

____

____

____

____

____

MY MONEY JOURNAL

August ____________

DATE	ITEM DESCRIPTION	I OWE YOU	YOU OWE ME	PAID

NOTES:

MY MONEY JOURNAL

August ____________

DATE	ITEM DESCRIPTION	I OWE YOU	YOU OWE ME	PAID

NOTES:

MY MONEY JOURNAL

August ________

DATE	ITEM DESCRIPTION	I OWE YOU	YOU OWE ME	PAID

NOTES:

MY MONEY JOURNAL

August ______________

DATE	ITEM DESCRIPTION	I OWE YOU	YOU OWE ME	PAID

NOTES:

MY MONEY JOURNAL

September ____________

DATE	ITEM DESCRIPTION	I OWE YOU	YOU OWE ME	PAID

NOTES:

MY MONEY JOURNAL

September ___________

DATE	ITEM DESCRIPTION	I OWE YOU	YOU OWE ME	PAID

NOTES:

MY MONEY JOURNAL

September ____________

DATE	ITEM DESCRIPTION	I OWE YOU	YOU OWE ME	PAID

NOTES:

MY MONEY JOURNAL

September ____________

DATE	ITEM DESCRIPTION	I OWE YOU	YOU OWE ME	PAID

NOTES:

____

____

____

____

____

____

MY MONEY JOURNAL

September ___________

DATE	ITEM DESCRIPTION	I OWE YOU	YOU OWE ME	PAID

NOTES:

MY MONEY JOURNAL

September ____________

DATE	ITEM DESCRIPTION	I OWE YOU	YOU OWE ME	PAID

NOTES:

MY MONEY JOURNAL

September ___________

DATE	ITEM DESCRIPTION	I OWE YOU	YOU OWE ME	PAID

NOTES:

MY MONEY JOURNAL

September ____________

DATE	ITEM DESCRIPTION	I OWE YOU	YOU OWE ME	PAID

NOTES:

MY MONEY JOURNAL

September ____________

DATE	ITEM DESCRIPTION	I OWE YOU	YOU OWE ME	PAID

NOTES:

____

____

____

____

____

____

MY MONEY JOURNAL

September ___________

DATE	ITEM DESCRIPTION	I OWE YOU	YOU OWE ME	PAID

NOTES:

MY MONEY JOURNAL

October ____________

DATE	ITEM DESCRIPTION	I OWE YOU	YOU OWE ME	PAID

NOTES:

____

____

____

____

____

____

MY MONEY JOURNAL

October ___________

DATE	ITEM DESCRIPTION	I OWE YOU	YOU OWE ME	PAID

NOTES:

MY MONEY JOURNAL

October ____________

DATE	ITEM DESCRIPTION	I OWE YOU	YOU OWE ME	PAID

NOTES:

MY MONEY JOURNAL

October ____________

DATE	ITEM DESCRIPTION	I OWE YOU	YOU OWE ME	PAID

NOTES:

____

____

____

____

____

____

MY MONEY JOURNAL

October ____________

DATE	ITEM DESCRIPTION	I OWE YOU	YOU OWE ME	PAID

NOTES:

____

____

____

____

____

____

MY MONEY JOURNAL

October ___________

DATE	ITEM DESCRIPTION	I OWE YOU	YOU OWE ME	PAID

NOTES:

MY MONEY JOURNAL

October ____________

DATE	ITEM DESCRIPTION	I OWE YOU	YOU OWE ME	PAID

NOTES:

MY MONEY JOURNAL

October ___________

DATE	ITEM DESCRIPTION	I OWE YOU	YOU OWE ME	PAID

NOTES:

MY MONEY JOURNAL

October ____________

DATE	ITEM DESCRIPTION	I OWE YOU	YOU OWE ME	PAID

NOTES:

____

____

____

____

____

____

MY MONEY JOURNAL

October ____________

DATE	ITEM DESCRIPTION	I OWE YOU	YOU OWE ME	PAID

NOTES:

MY MONEY JOURNAL

November ____________

DATE	ITEM DESCRIPTION	I OWE YOU	YOU OWE ME	PAID

NOTES:

MY MONEY JOURNAL

November ____________

DATE	ITEM DESCRIPTION	I OWE YOU	YOU OWE ME	PAID

NOTES:

MY MONEY JOURNAL

November ____________

DATE	ITEM DESCRIPTION	I OWE YOU	YOU OWE ME	PAID

NOTES:

MY MONEY JOURNAL

November ____________

DATE	ITEM DESCRIPTION	I OWE YOU	YOU OWE ME	PAID

NOTES:

MY MONEY JOURNAL

November ____________

DATE	ITEM DESCRIPTION	I OWE YOU	YOU OWE ME	PAID

NOTES:

MY MONEY JOURNAL

November ____________

DATE	ITEM DESCRIPTION	I OWE YOU	YOU OWE ME	PAID

NOTES:

____

____

____

____

____

____

MY MONEY JOURNAL

November ____________

DATE	ITEM DESCRIPTION	I OWE YOU	YOU OWE ME	PAID

NOTES:

MY MONEY JOURNAL

November ____________

DATE	ITEM DESCRIPTION	I OWE YOU	YOU OWE ME	PAID

NOTES:

____

____

____

____

____

____

MY MONEY JOURNAL

November ____________

DATE	ITEM DESCRIPTION	I OWE YOU	YOU OWE ME	PAID

NOTES:

____

____

____

____

____

____

MY MONEY JOURNAL

November ___________

DATE	ITEM DESCRIPTION	I OWE YOU	YOU OWE ME	PAID

NOTES:

MY MONEY JOURNAL

December ____________

DATE	ITEM DESCRIPTION	I OWE YOU	YOU OWE ME	PAID

NOTES:

MY MONEY JOURNAL

December ____________

DATE	ITEM DESCRIPTION	I OWE YOU	YOU OWE ME	PAID

NOTES:

MY MONEY JOURNAL

December ___________

DATE	ITEM DESCRIPTION	I OWE YOU	YOU OWE ME	PAID

NOTES:

___

___

___

___

___

___

MY MONEY JOURNAL

December ___________

DATE	ITEM DESCRIPTION	I OWE YOU	YOU OWE ME	PAID

NOTES:

MY MONEY JOURNAL

December ______________

DATE	ITEM DESCRIPTION	I OWE YOU	YOU OWE ME	PAID

NOTES:

____

____

____

____

____

____

MY MONEY JOURNAL

December ___________

DATE	ITEM DESCRIPTION	I OWE YOU	YOU OWE ME	PAID

NOTES:

MY MONEY JOURNAL

December ____________

DATE	ITEM DESCRIPTION	I OWE YOU	YOU OWE ME	PAID

NOTES:

____

____

____

____

____

____

MY MONEY JOURNAL

December ____________

DATE	ITEM DESCRIPTION	I OWE YOU	YOU OWE ME	PAID

NOTES:

____

____

____

____

____

____

MY MONEY JOURNAL

December ____________

DATE	ITEM DESCRIPTION	I OWE YOU	YOU OWE ME	PAID

NOTES:

____

____

____

____

____

____

MY MONEY JOURNAL

December ____________

DATE	ITEM DESCRIPTION	I OWE YOU	YOU OWE ME	PAID

NOTES:

Made in the USA
Monee, IL
04 November 2026

67375784R00069